T0011101

Little Stars
HOCKEY

A CRABTREE SEEDLINGS BOOK

Buffy Silverman

CRABTREE
PUBLISHING COMPANY
WWW.CRABTREEBOOKS.COM

I am on a
hockey team.

helmet

4

I wear gloves and a **helmet** to stay safe.

5

Thick pads **protect** my shoulders, elbows, and legs.

We learn to skate fast.

8

We use our hockey sticks to move the **puck**.

hockey stick

puck

11

Each team tries to get the puck into the other team's **goal**.

We stop, pass, and shoot the puck.

14

The **goaltender** guards the net and tries to keep the puck out.

My team shoots the puck into the net.

19

We score a point!

Glossary

goal (gohl): A goal is scored when a player shoots the puck into the other team's net. A team gets one point for each goal. The net with its frame is also called a goal.

goaltender (gohl-TEN-dur): A goaltender is the player whose job is to keep the puck out of the goal.

helmet (HEL-mit): A helmet covers a player's head and protects it from injuries.

hockey (HOK-ee): Hockey is a game played on ice with two teams. Each team tries to score goals by shooting a puck into the other team's net.

protect (pruh-TEKT): To keep something safe from harm.

puck (PUCK): The puck is a hard rubber disk that players hit with their hockey sticks.

Index

School-to-Home Support for Caregivers and Teachers

Crabtree Seedlings books help children grow by letting them practice reading. Here are a few guiding questions to help the reader build his or her comprehension skills. Possible answers are included.

Before Reading

- **What do I think this book is about?** I think this book is about playing hockey. It might tell us the rules of the game.

- **What do I want to learn about this topic?** I want to learn about the equipment that a hockey player wears.

During Reading

- **I wonder why...** I wonder why the goaltender wears different pads than the players.

- **What have I learned so far?** I learned that hockey players wear gloves, helmets, pads, and skates.

After Reading

- **What details did I learn about this topic?** I learned that hockey players use hockey sticks to move the puck around the ice and into the other team's goal.

- **Write down unfamiliar words and ask questions to help understand their meaning.** I see the word *protect* on page 6 and the word *goal* on page 13. The other vocabulary words are listed on pages 22 and 23.

Library and Archives Canada Cataloguing in Publication

Title: Little stars hockey / Buffy Silverman.
Other titles: Hockey
Names: Silverman, Buffy, author.
Description: Series statement: Little stars | "A Crabtree seedlings book". | Includes index. |
  Previously published in electronic format by Blue Door Education in 2020.
Identifiers: Canadiana 20200378910 | ISBN 9781427129802 (hardcover) | ISBN 9781427129987 (softcover)
Subjects: LCSH: Hockey—Juvenile literature.
Classification: LCC GV847.25 .S54 2021 | DDC j796.962—dc23

Library of Congress Cataloging-in-Publication Data

Names: Silverman, Buffy, author.
Title: Little stars hockey / Buffy Silverman.
Other titles: Hockey
Description: New York, NY : Crabtree Publishing Company, [2021] | Series: Little stars: a Crabtree seedlings book | Includes index.
Identifiers: LCCN 2020049311 | ISBN 9781427129802 (hardcover) | ISBN 9781427129987 (paperback)
Subjects: LCSH: Hockey--Juvenile literature.
Classification: LCC GV847.25 .S492 2021 | DDC 796.356--dc23
LC record available at https://lccn.loc.gov/2020049311

Crabtree Publishing Company
www.crabtreebooks.com   1–800–387–7650

e-book ISBN 978-1-947632-28-8

Print book version produced jointly with Blue Door Education in 2021

Written by Buffy Silverman

Production coordinator and Prepress technician: Samara Parent

Print coordinator: Katherine Berti

Printed in the U.S.A./012021/CG20201102

Photo credits: Cover © Click Images; p2-3 © Sergei Butorin; p5 © Valeriy Lebedev; page 6 © Dardalnna; page 8-9 © Click Images; page 10-11 © Vanessa van Rensburg; page 12 © Lucky Business; page 15 and 16 © Click Images; page 18-19 © Lucky Business; page 20 © Stankevich
All photos from Shutterstock.com

Published in Canada
Crabtree Publishing
616 Welland Ave.
St. Catharines, Ontario
L2M 5V6

Published in the United States
Crabtree Publishing
347 Fifth Ave.
Suite 1402-145
New York, NY 10016

Published in the United Kingdom
Crabtree Publishing
Maritime House
Basin Road North, Hove
BN41 1WR

Published in Australia
Crabtree Publishing
Unit 3 – 5 Currumbin Court
Capalaba
QLD 4157